THE FEE FOR EXALTATION

Library and Archives Canada Cataloguing in Publication

Tyndall, John, 1951-
     The fee for exaltation / John Tyndall.
Poems.
ISBN 978-0-88753-435-5
     I. Title.

PS8589.Y5F43 2007   C811'.54   C2007-904114-0

Thanks to Diane, Arthur, Kristen, and Dad; Cathy and Jean Cleave; Verna
Dougall; Lenore Keeshig-Tobias; *The Wiarton Echo*; Allan Bartley; Wilbert
Logan; Cynthia Norris; Sandra O'Hagan; the members of the group; my edi-
tor, John B. Lee; and all at Black Moss Press.

An earlier version of "Arizona Dead or Alive" appeared in *Henry's Creature:
Poems and Stories on the Automobile*, edited by Roger Bell and John B. Lee
(Black Moss Press, 2000).

The Palm Poets Series is published by Black Moss Press at 2450 Byng Road,
Windsor, Ontario N8W 3E8.

Black Moss would like to acknowledge the generous support of the Canada
Council and the Ontario Arts Council for its publishing program.

Le Conseil des Arts | The Canada Council
du Canada | for the Arts

ONTARIO ARTS COUNCIL
CONSEIL DES ARTS DE L'ONTARIO

THE FEE FOR EXALTATION

JOHN TYNDALL

For my father, Guy Christian Tyndall
and to the memory of my mother, Helen Christianna Matthews.

I

Mother

"So I just got to tell you
Goodbye Goodbye"
John Lennon

At Every Knell

Now I dread the klaxon blare
of long...short.short long-distance calls
not a single mellifluous ring
not the chiming sound of bells
but a rise and fall   a rise and fall
like an ambulance siren after midnight
announces news of my mother's stroke
hello her left side is paralysed
hello her speech is silence
hello her eyes are motionless
oh she can move her arm
oh she can walk again
oh she gave us a dirty look
since her voice still cannot speak

How I dread long-distance calls

Even the latest good God tidings
do not erase the fears I feel
at every knell I want to kneel

Out of Balance

Father says Mother sees
a rabbit on the lawn
Right there   Right there
even when he stands
in the exact place
she swears she sees
a woman and a man
Over here   Over here
under combined attacks
glaucoma   Parkinson's   stroke
congestive heart failure
under combined influences
eye-drops   diuretics   dopa
rat-poison-blood-thinners
who would not hallucinate
eyes\brain out of balance
as doctors dither
over drug dosages
who would not see rabbits
who would not miss the fox
outstretched on the lawn

10

Closed Circuit

Mother rested shaded from sunshine
wheelchair flush with patio table
drank cold water left-handed
until she emptied her plastic cup
then she raised drained vessel
again and again to puckered lip
and when I took it away
broke her closed circuit of sip
she lifted my sister's black purse
to her mouth like a wineskin
tilted back her gray-haired head
even into dazzle-bright sunlight
to receive any lingering drip
and when I took it away
she hoisted hand to parched lip
again and again a ghostly glass
closed her short circuit of sip

Aftershocks

In the wake of Mother's major stroke
as care restored her motion
rebuilt her speech word by word by word
how complacent our family grew
with expectations of progress
clearing away rubble from pathways
manoeuvring downed limbs with walker or cane
so surprised we watched her slide into
immobility   incomprehension   incontinence
back to the hospital to the geriatric ward
where damaged ones slap the coded door
where food becomes plaything or face-paint
where cranial x-rays like a seismograph
reveal traces of two earth-shattering events
aftershocks that felled the unwitting innocent
tremors that shook Mother's soul to stillness

Morning Fog

Out of nighttime darkness Mom
awoke into daytimeless mist
no discernable difference between
nocturnal and diurnal rhythms
each moment wound tight by her wounds
fixed to the sweep of nursing's clock
and as late Summer degraded
toward an early Fall I despaired
resigned with my wife and my son
that his Nana's night-days on Earth
numbered fewer and fewer and fewer
when one Sunday she dawned
repaired neural nets   gathered thought
blood-sacred vessels poured life anew
she spoke clearly   moved freely
as though a morning fog had lifted
and she was here and she knew
the light within her and without her

II

Arid Zone A

Toronto airport
beverage billboard points Right
Here > Arizona.

The Girl on Flight 683
(Toronto to Phoenix)

The window seat is wasted
on the girl beside me.
As our jet taxies to the runway
she glares straight ahead in fright
refuses gum with shaken head
remains sepulchrally silent.
We begin our take-off surge.
In her mind we are already dead
consumed by inferno
burnt offerings to unholy gods
or burst in air too thin
for breath, too cold for life
or plunged through ocean depths
in minute food-chain pieces
or crushed against the earth
a new flesh-and-metal matrix.
Not the in-flight movie
nor carbonated drinks
nor a hot meal
nor our Captain's word
of balmy Phoenix weather
brings her soul relief.
We descend to desert.
Her fears rise as cruel
and complex as air traffic.
Our wheels touch down
and I wonder if death
will end her dread
of coming from and going to.

Dips and Washes

Slip away on Carefree Highway
you will see a sign

      DIP

and indeed the road
falls into a broad gully
rises on the other side
of baked landscape.

Further west looms
another warning

      WATCH
      FOR
      WATER
      ON
      ROAD

and you may start to laugh
surrounded by Arizona sand
sun scorching at zenith
moisture a hazy memory.

But like markings on Mars
from a recent celestial era
trace the liquid flow
you must believe the signs

> FLASH
> FLOOD
> AREA

> IMPASSABLE
> DURING
> HIGH
> WATER

for the dips and washes
like sidewinder slither
follow sinuate trails
across a terrain
scoured at intervals
by intemperate fury

the desert monsoon.

19

Los Brazeletes

For Herb Kauhl

With our walking sticks
last year's flower-stalks
cut from yucca plants
with these desiccated pieces
of the Sonoran Desert
we climb St. Clair Mountain
Tonto National Forest
of prickly pear and teddy bear
barrel and saguaro cacti
able to pierce shoe leather
or rubber soles at will.

No thick underbrush
chokes this arid zone
we step in the spaces
between water-hoarding growth
trod the granite, sandstone, schist
imbedded in the caliche
dried as hard as chalk
lean upon our third-leg staffs
to a first summit spur
where our shadows fall
invisible on an ancient spring
afar in the valley below.

Along a razorback ridge the trail
leads to a second peak
crowned by *Los Brazeletes*
ruins named after beads
drilled   polished   discarded
along with potsherds centuries ago
and while we know the Hohokam
built here above the spring
within sight of the Verde River
to command the entire panorama
why did they abandon this eyrie
to the dark hawk circling overhead?

We might fathom a drought
lasting a span of years
seek answers to questions
of conservation and ration
but in the face of decades
how soon would we pitch
our plastic bottles and leave?

We scramble descent
past curve and curve
of tortuous saguaro arms
pointing us away, away
as late-morning climbers
follow guides upward

until down at mountain's base
we discover new relics
littered .22 and .357 magnum shells.

I pick up two brazen casings
and blow our farewell whistles
to the spirits and the hawk above.

Zeno's Eire

Down the desert road
from quiet Carefree
Cave Creek is littered
with tourist snares
baited with shot glasses
newly-shipped artifacts
t-shirt skeletons leering
"but it's a dry heat"
so the hole-in-the-wall haven
of Zeno's Book Barn
shocks the poet alive
almost five thousand miles
from Phoenix Park, Dublin
to discover *Finnegans Wake*
hardcover, fine
Heaney's *Station Island*
paperback, pristine
where ALP the sacred riverrun
never ran down to the sea
where Sweeney-bird never ever
flew treetop to outcrop
even here in Arizona
the bardic, shameless, joyous
voices of Eire
resound.

Arizona Dead or Alive

White-tailed doe dead
by the roadside
her head wound still bright
red as liquid sunrise
her body left behind
along with two crashed cars
her spirit right behind
the eyes of shocked humans
milling about shattered glass
caught in the swirling glare
ambulance and police cruisers
crimson round and round.

*

This coyote stretched so still
on unforgiving pavement
stiff in the heat of noon
no more with midnight pack
padding through arroyos
scaling dry hard banks
to sing down the moon and stars
no more with kin
plotting their fathers' trail
seeking their mothers' course
to chorus revenge upon rival clans
and scorn upon owners of cats.

*

At the infinite instant
between vapour-cold night
and muzzle-warm morning
when pure colour returns
to spiny cacti and spindly bush
in the ancient desert hush
a *palo verde* speaks
in tongues of warning
hidden snorts and grunts
a porky trinity of *javelinas*
father and mother and offspring
ready their trotters or tusks.

Sedona

In my mother's Carefree kitchen
she shakes her good right hand
speaks her impassioned mind

You - go - to - Sedona
I - go - to - Sedona.

She will risk health
at higher altitudes
to see her favourite Arizona
monuments in red, red stone

Cathedral Rock, Bell Rock
and her dearest
Coffeepot Rock.

Mother and Father and I
climb by car north
out of Sonoran Desert
leave cactus behind
mount mesa after mesa
even glimpse snow-peaks
before we arrive at Sedona.

Every vista, every vantage
surreal beauty
surfeit of humanity.

But I am able to forgive those
who die to live in this place
whose dwellings swell like waves
around the blood-hued rocks

when I hear my father
speechless with awe
when I see my mother
blinding with grace.

27

The Woman on Flight 684
(Phoenix to Toronto)

We share a cabin window.

We rise out of desert heat
shimmering above terminals
watch landscapes gyre
beneath mythic silver wings.
She is named Helen
like my mother
one of light, of sun
a ray, a beam.
Her heart flies upon laughter.
We share family lore
black sheep
links of generation
loves, losses.

She counsels bereaved
on death, on dying
serenity salted and sly.
She revels in drink, in food
movies flicker within her eyes.

We know our return flight
to northern homes
to lovers and children
familiar, unknown
will unfold as it will unfold.

III

Rhymes with Orangeman

My grandfather, Arthur Tyndall,
was a loyal Orangeman,
descendant of followers
of the Red Hand of Ulster,
the Sword and the Horse of Orange.

Tyndall Family Tree

William T. [only child] m. Emelia Bryne
1766-1823   1768-1802

       |

John T. [third child] m. Sarah Macassey
1792-1847   1793?-1867

       |

John T. [second child] m. Louisa Hamilton
1820-1893   1845-1940
The scientist.

          |

John T. [second child] m. Ethel Brinkman
1873-1942   1879-1963
 Donated land for
 L.O.L. 1723

          |

Joseph T. [fifth child] m. Jane ?
1799-1836

          |

Thomas T. [first child] m. Harriet Watchorn
1822-1873   1825-1875

          |

Thomas T. [first child] m. Mary Christian
1846-1908   1846-1926

          |

Arthur T. [sixth child] m. Lillian McKinley
1885-1969   1891-1970

          |

Guy T. [second child] m. Helen Matthews
 1918-   1921-1999

          |

John T. [second child] m. Diane Halpin
1951-   1952-
The author.

          |

Arthur T. [only child]
1989-

Digging Potatoes (I.)

Digging potatoes with Dad
unearthed tubers multiply
ancient Peruvian staple
cultivated in Ireland
then in Canada by my
Orange Lodge grandfather
his father before him
his father before
labour transplanted
with old hatreds
we fork rich soil
harvest edible links
in our family history
my own story
watching grandfather
hill his potatoes
hoe his perfect rows
fill his root cellar
the starchy stuff
nourishes all alike
friend or foe

Father to Son

I.

My great-great-great-grandfather
Joseph Henry Tyndall died
aboard ship bound for Canada
leaving home at Prospect Hall
Coolcullen, Co. Kilkenny, Ireland
in the year of Our Lord 1836.

A decade before the Great Famine
he and his brother Anthony
and both their families fled
bringing Orange rites
to the new promised land
when Joseph was committed
consumed and scattered by currents
under the weight of green water.

II.

My great-great-grandfather
Thomas William Tyndall arrived.

Rhymes with Orangeman

found
Loyal Orange Association of British America
Rules of the Royal Scarlet Order
Constitution and Laws.
Toronto: Sentinel, 1915. "Revised to date."

Hymns to accompany Ritual
Secret Work
Worshipful Master
Exaltation to Royal Scarlet
King William III., Prince of Orange
pure religion
Union Jack

Protestant Briton
at home, in the farthest parts of the world
misunderstood, and by others misrepresented
the history of parties in Ireland
suppress rebellion, repel invasion
The Altar and the Throne
Covenant of Freedom
when they themselves are called hence

clipped
obituary 1969, *The Echo*
Arthur Robert Tyndall, 83, was a member of the Dyers
Bay L.O.L. 1723

owned
Proud People: The Lindsay Township History Book
Compiled by the Lindsay Township Historical Society,
1987

The Orange Lodge came to Dyers Bay
a 24-by-36-foot floor plan
set on a stone foundation
"that we have a bee for to get some wood"
"that three lamp chimbly be got"

Orange Young Britons
loyalty to Queen and country
See "Offences" and "Trials"
Offences. Marrying Roman Catholic
not to leave Lodge without permission
candidate engaged in sale of liquor, barred
bore binge man
who shall compose the Grand Lodge
resolved, declared and enacted
fines for frivolous and vexatious complaints
more whinge man

warrant for Loyal Orange Lodge 1723 issued on October 27, 1899
to Thomas Tyndall
John Christian Tyndall married Ethel Brinkman.
Ladies' Orange Benevolent Association
Mother crossed herself, mocking, "Spectacles, testicles, wallet and watch."
John C. Tyndall and his wife sold one-half acre
to L.O.L. 1723 for $6

Celebrations — 12th July
the real event
the Orange Day parade and picnic
Where on the Twelfth, I'll proudly wear
"that we send invitations to Spry, Stokes Bay and Tobermory
to come to Dyers Bay to celebrate"
and Arthur Tyndall so well-known for his booming voice
And it's on the Twelfth I'll proudly wear

for the settlers who took up land in the area
during the 1880s and 1890s
holding certificates in the Benefit Fund
ipso facto revived and renewed
the largest sum or the longest date
Penalty for Non-Payment

he shall pay assessments according to his age
and of those who have failed to pay
deemed guilty of a violation of his trust
a member not in good standing loses all

issue of delinquent dues was a common one
a brother in arrears
core cringe man
suspension or expulsion
the Grand Master shall summon a meeting
custodian of the seals
a brother affiliating from Ireland
the three black ball rule
"cancelled by death"

Brethren from Ireland
Sir Knight and Brother
a list of the suspensions and expulsions
Scribe of the Illustrious Order
the Orange, Purple, Blue and Royal Arch Purple degrees
the fee for exaltation
give the retiring password
reasons for refusing to recommend the brother
nor dinge man
shall be designated "Worshipful"

Sir Knight Companion Inward Herald
the second Tuesday in January
a burnt or defaced Dispensation
sore singe man

an application for affiliation as well as for initiation
notwithstanding his previous failure to comply
"What was your age last birthday?"
(in case of death)
and in red ink the words set out
expectancy of life is hereby fixed
in accordance with resolutions adopted
members leaving for the seat of war
And when I'm on the ocean I hope for me you'll pray.
**no mention at this meeting of impending war
or at the next meeting, August 29, 1914, of actual war**

Grand Master of the Province
shall, without delay, investigate and correct
a majority of two-thirds of the members
on such extra-hazardous occupation
cartridges, shells, gunpowder, dynamite
all persons who have suffered the loss of an arm, or a leg, or an eye
from any unavoidable cause

your twinge man
a member changes his place of residence
neglects his duty
death by suicide, or at the hands of the law

the good government of the lodge
duly attested, proving the death
clothed in the regalia provided
wore tinge man
upon complying
a parade for Divine Service
The Outside Tyler shall guard the entrance
door hinge man

Closing the Lodge with Prayer
Sir Knights wear Scarlet sashes
trimmed with Orange silk fringe or gold fringe
It was worn at Derry, Aughrim, Enniskillen and the Boyne.
the Rose, Thistle, Shamrock and Maple Leaves entwined,
richly trimmed

for fringe man
The Sash My Father Wore
and we pray, when so formed
And it will always be as now
in 1960 and 1961
before the lodge disintegrated completely
assets of $25 and liabilities of $4
L.O.L. 1723's extinction was inevitable

Notify the Worshipful Master
Summons for a Trial of a Member
For marrying a Roman Catholic
I, John Charles Tyndall
married Diane Halpin, 1986
+Marie+Diane+Thérèse+Olive+Halpin+
Mother warned, "If religion becomes an issue, drop it like a hot potato."
you are summoned and required to attend
proceeded against for violation of his obligation
Fac Simile Grand Master's Signature
after due trial and conviction
Wife's Religion
Absence of Defendant or Complainant From Trial
Evidence to be Taken in Writing
brother is pronounced guilty

Four Times Removed

When I learned to read
I thought I'd found myself
in Webster's New World Dictionary
College Edition, page 1576
Tyndall, John, 1820-1893
British physicist
where I printed
*That's **MY** name*
wondering for years
if we were related
and now at fifty-one
almost the age he first married
I know that his father, John
and my great-great-great-grandfather, Joseph
were brothers, making me
his first cousin
four times removed
this Professor of Natural Philosophy
in the Royal Institution
of Great Britain
this co-conspirator in the X Club
exalting science over religion
this propounder of
what do they write?
Materialistic Transcendence?

this Alpine mountaineer
who looked to Germany
for his higher education
as William Tyndale
had looked for religious reform
John, who stormed the bastions
of the United Kingdom's churches
both Catholic and Protestant
befriending and defending Darwin
and even if he courted a coterie
of female science worshippers
Lothario of the lecture circuit
experiments and books remain
forever sky is Tyndall blue
and while I scan and cut up
four of his many texts
with the ghost of William S. Burroughs
peeking over my shoulder
refract his words
through prisms
I promise my cousin
I will never parody
Heat Considered as a Mode of Motion
although I so yearn to describe
Meat as a Mode of Motion.

S(L)ight Plays upon Works by Cousin John, Scientist

John Tyndall
b. August 2, 1820
d. December 4, 1893
The Belfast Address, 1874
imagine the Bishop
after hearing this
to allow
consideration
after due reflection
himself by
contemplation of the facts
and which
given even adverse reasonings
due weight
to proceed thus
the Bishop's reasoning
unanswerable
imitation
a product of his age
the nature of the soul
a topic of the students
to know the leanings
at once requested
upon the soul

Bishop Butler the question
only agitated
by the clear-witted
their best arguments
to brutes and men
this character
admitted it
boldly embraced
his scheme of immortality

**LL.D., F.R.S.,
AUTHOR OF "FRAGMENTS OF SCIENCE
FOR UNSCIENTIFIC PEOPLE," "HEAT
AS A MODE OF MOTION," ETC.,
ETC.
Hours of Exercise in the Alps, 1871
Chapter XIII
the glacier and the adjacent heights
an attempt
by the flank of the mountain
we reached
the ice cascade
sky was clear and the air
ascended**

swiftest necromancy
a peculiar degree
clouds suddenly generated
drifting up the valley
swathing the mountain-tops
clear for a time
grandeur is conceded
but the higher snow-fields
are altogether beautiful
endowed with
the loveliness of woman
the day was one
wrought by the cloud-filled
the top
might be felt
the vision
the darkness
the deep blue heaven
the dazzling snows
the black and craggy summit
other summits and other crags
in succession
whirl
into infinite haze

On Sound, 1867
Chapter VI
musical flames
burst spontaneously into song
exceedingly intense
a ring burner
a tin tube
flame flutters at first
chastens its impulses
deep and clear musical tone
lowering the gas
caused to cease
silence, another note
the fundamental
first harmonic
the aerial column
still more striking
a totally different purpose
a steady stand
hear the incipient flutter
the more powerful sound
becomes more violent
a storm of music
suddenly ceased
into extinction
relight the flame
when raised
again sings

one of the harmonics
the note
the storm
bursts forth
hurricane of sound
by lowering the flame
note is abolished
hear the first harmonic
flame still smaller
the second is heard
ears being disciplined
once more fully on
the deepest note
the harmonics
struggling
amid the general uproar
becomes powerful
to shake the floor
while the extinction
of the sonorous pulses
announces
an explosion
it must occur
a tube of this kind
the roar of a flame
music

Defence, Vindication
Apology for the Belfast Address, 1874
My critic commits this mistake
that I am struggling
experiences the most exquisite pleasures
holding me down
as if his imagination
were equally real
his picture
a mere delusion
I do not struggle
do not fear the charge of Atheism
do not even disavow it
any definition of the Supreme
his order would be likely to frame

48

be so grand as it is now. *of the star is quenched at* **in the midst of** and palaeontologist till they are filled, and *between the bright beads* **astound all** depths to the **of height and depth** *extinction. Now, our singing* **appear to me** the sea-bottoms of **Alpine scenery depends.** *When it begins to sing you* **public tolerance for** the leaves of that stone and deep-cut gorges we *motion which may be analyzed* **for the statement of** know, stamped the **dotted with dreary islands** *an opera-glass, as in the case* **views, views** *more in* and surer than those **mountain-tops** *the image of this flame in a* **verities which science** of history, which **at the waste of energy** geology, with its **and which many** into abysses of past **men over things** regarding the life **I thought, welcome** which the periods **say it without** having been created. **relief** Butler ceased to have **attention of enlightened** conceptions has been *ruby and emerald in the lower* **ages it was forced to slide** *about the fripperies* mind being rendered *a piece of looking-glass so* by the ice itself are so **verbal quibbles of** of the idea that not *image of such a star, on tilting* slippery that it is impossible **the forcing on the** for sixty thousand, *the line of light obtained will* their inclination is at all **Pilgrimages; the** thousand, but for aeons *form a string of coloured beads* world it must have been **epochs from the definition** millions of years, this *effect is obtained when an* **filled! We can** restore **Conception; the** theatre of life and *star and shaken.* *This* thought, and in doing so **Divine Glories of the** the rocks has been *act of twinkling the light* **which now lifts its pinnacle** from subcambrian **Sacred Heart - standing** *intervals; the dark spaces* **in those days could not** deposits thickening over **these chimeras, which** *corresponding to the periods of* **Pour ice into those valleys** today. And upon **thinking men, it did not** *flame is twinkling flame.* **you eliminate those contrasts** book are, as you **extravagant to claim the** *observe a certain quivering* on which the grandeur of characters, plainer **an hour and a half,** *with*

49

looking-glass, or **Instead of skiey pinnacles** formed by the ink
more reasonable *of the star. I can now see* **should have an**
icy sea carry the mind back ***accordance with the*** *small*
looking-glass. On tilting **formed by the highest** time, compared
with **has brought to light,** astounding revelations
religious teachers; which satisfied Bishop ***weary souls***
would, of the ancient earth, ***on the part of good*** a
visual angle ***with gratification and*** The rigidity of old
unworthy, if I may The rocks thus polished *Alps, the*
alternate flash of relaxed, the public ***discourtesy, of the***
exceedingly smooth and *and larger stars. If you place* gradually
tolerant ***heathens; the fight*** to stand on them where
that you can see in it the for six thousand, nor ***of Ritualism,***
and the considerable. But what a *the glass quickly to and*
fro, nor for six thousand ***the Athanasian Creed*** when
the valleys were thus *not be continuous, but will* embracing
untold ***public view of Pontigny*** the state of things
in *of extreme beauty. The same* earth has been the ***dating of***
historic we submerge many a mass *opera-glass is pointed*
to the death. The riddle of ***of the Immaculate*** skyward.
Switzerland *experiment shows that in the* read by the geologist
proclamation of the

Here, however, I touch a theme
too great for me to handle, but
which will assuredly be handled
by the loftiest minds, when you and I,
like streaks of morning cloud,
shall have melted into the infinite
azure of the past.

the mountain ridge
torn asunder
the sun play a wild
mystic music

musical flames
analysis of musical flame
vibration of flame
harmonic sounds of flame
extraneous sounds on flame
sensitive naked flames
fish-tail and bat's-wing flames
flames from circular apertures
sensitiveness
pitch
the vowel-flame
sensitive smoke-jets
sensitive water-jets
naked flames

the Roman Catholic Church
call gluttony a mortal sin?
fasting occupy a place
in the disciplines of religion?
there is moral and religious virtue
even in a hydro-carbon?

52

Pinning the Tail

You are lucky, Jim
that Art is out tonight.

My grampa, Art Tyndall
was the last Orangeman
of our line, our clan
he swore off liquor
enrager of all souls
imagine how much farther
soused-in-his-cups-drunk
he would have flung
his daughter Kathy's beau
he marched and played music
on the Twelfth of July
in Dyers Bay his first home
but soon graced a church pew
in post-war Wiarton
where he transformed himself
escarpment hard
to cedar supple
when Jean his younger daughter
fell in love, fell in love
with James Plourde
sweet-whistling son
of French-Canadian Catholics

and Art put away
his Orange buttons
In Glorious, Pious & Immortal
Memory of King William III
and Jim pinned one
In Memoriam tail-on
his own Canadian Club ass
flying the twisted fringe.

Mon Dieu!

A thousand miles across Canada
Mémère Halpin, matriarch
of my lover's clan
calls her first grandchild
her first granddaughter
concerning rumours
a new beau in 1984
my forename, John
impresses, the same
as her departed husband's
but when she learns
my Christian family name
four hundred and fifty years
after Thomas More ranted
a strong heretic
and worthy to be burnt
seven hundred and fifty thousand
words of damnation
strangulation and immolation
upon my ancestor William
Mémère exclaims, *Mon Dieu!*
Ce n'est pas un nom catholique.

Archbishop Uncle Charles

I.

Diane and I flew
to Saskatchewan
for a family wedding
and stayed rooms apart
in the official residence
of The Most Reverend Charles Halpin
Archbishop of Regina
His Excellency
her uncle
and I gave him a gift
a bottle of single-malt scotch
from the Valley of the Deer
and he drank and I drank
and he drank and he drank
and I slept under the attic
close to the scary-boo room
Diane's brothers swore
was haunted and was haunted
by the priestly regalia
by the holy wedding Mass
by the scared *hibou*
stuffed in the dining-room
by our talk of my intentions
vis-à-vis his favourite niece
whose marriage he would celebrate
at her long-ago
little girl
request

II.

Uncle Charles flew
to London, Ontario
to marry Diane and me
he, a canon lawyer
who could shuffle paper
for a marriage between Catholic
and United Church partners
agreed to readings from both
New Jerusalem and King James Bibles
agreed to dispense with Mass
for the sake of ecumenicalism
and while Diane prepared for nuptials
at her matron-of-honour's home
His Excellency visited me
at our openly common-law apartment
on the hunt for paraphernalia
a glass dish and blue silk
to hold our golden rings
a ceramic bowl
and a sprinkler for holy water
to bless our covenant
and when we had found everything
he tested the sprinkler
splashing tap-water
in my face

It works

The Recovering Catholic

My friend, the recovering Catholic
remembers the guilt, the guilt
nun teachers charting
the pie-graph of a soul
slices of venial sin
versus mortal sins
he remembers confessing
false omissions and commissions
rather than real emissions
crossing himself
In the name of the Father
skip the Son
over the fence
and you're done
but he never stole
the sacristy wine
serving as an altar-boy
a deathbed loophole
foreseen in dream
sinking in green water
deep and deeper

darker

down

Pagan Poet

Everything is real
swimming in Zen pools
every lap a cool journey
there and back, again and again
but I cannot remember
the slope of sacred water
never christened, never baptized
neither Protestant nor Catholic
so our marriage remains covenant
but could be sacrament
retroactively upon my immersion
in the name of the holy trinity
until then my ultimate destination
the first circle of hell
not the darkest pit
knocking funny bones
with virtuous pagans
the poets Virgil and Horace
will welcome my melancholy
trying to step around
unbaptized infants
and while my son Arthur
received the light of Christ
he lives unconfirmed
never partaking

of the body or blood
but with or without
my faith in the Father
whether I wear my Irish cross
from Advent to Easter
or my fossil pendant
from Summer Solstice
to Autumn Equinox
I love Marie, mother Mary
Diane, huntress of the moon
Thérèse, pierced by arrows
Olive, branch of peace
Halpin, mountain of God
and

60

she loves me, she loves me
she loves me, she loves me

this I know

July 12, 2003

On the glorious twelfth
I witnessed a Catholic wedding
in Sacred Heart Church, Walkerton
under the eyes of Mary
Joseph and infant Jesus
called to the Eucharist
I crossed arms
over profane heart
received a blessing
from the groom's mother
in the name of Father
Son and Holy Spirit

As pilgrim day
gave way to festive night
on the O'Hagan farm
the sky blushed
to a sailor's delight
then over white tent
filled with revellers, drinkers
of water and wine
the full moon graced
each singular soul
with all glory
and honour

Digging Potatoes (II.)

Digging potatoes with Dad
we compost the unused
broken rotten stems
browned wrinkled leaves
distant cousins of deadly nightshade
we give back apples of earth to earth
some of her *pommes de terre*
nourish the future
regenerate
the generations
my only child
Arthur
my grandfather's namesake
plays *The Ode to Joy*
on Cynthia's silver flute
not *The Protestant Boys*
on the old Orange fife

IV

My Mummy's Dead

"I can't explain
so much pain"
John Lennon

Broken

There was a woman   named Helen Christianna
daughter of Emily Ferguson   and Burton Matthews
who lived by a lake   with her husband, Guy
he cared for her   after she fell
and only half of her   got up again
so she needed a walker   needed its wheels
or every journey   no matter the distance
was fraught with danger   from a stumble, a trip
thus it befell   early one summer
she tried to walk   zig-zag from couch to table
and she teetered   landing on her hip
which, broken   sent her to hospital
and thence to another   larger hospital
by the Owen Sound   where she had convalesced
three years earlier   undergoing physical therapy
for the half-body   that refused motion
and speech therapy   for the voice
that sometimes blurted   *This is my son*
and sometimes whispered   witless words
and there she lay   recovering strength
when blood in her brain   burst through again

'Sblood

you behold blood
on your mother's lips
smears of her life
spilt by infection
easily treated
by medicinal swabs
mouth as clinically clean
as the hospital sheets
she who split your heart
who once threatened
I'll smash you through the window
whose last words
when you promised you'd return
to her starched bedside
feebly breathed
'kay

your creator
is mortal
she who birthed you in gore

Room 304

We moved Mother
back to her hometown
Wiarton Hospital
in the high summer
her room, 304
around the corridor
from a stained glass story
by Lenore Keeshig-Tobias
how the pebbles
Nanabush threw in the air
became butterflies
tempting the infant people
to stand for the first time
and grow

On the wall at the foot
of her final resting-bed
there hung a reproduction
of Coffeepot Rock
her favourite formation
from red, red Sedona

Her window
on the courtyard
framed the same sky
the very light
she knew from birth
shone upon birch trees
soaring herring gulls
white butterfly clouds

Conducting Chopin

We play Mother's music
while awake she sleeps
in hospital gown

When I arrive today
Nakai's bird-bone flute
echoes around mesas
in the far Southwest
his primal notes fade

I cue another cassette
her favourite Chopin
12 Études, Opus 10
Number 3 in E major
Lento, ma non troppo

With my left hand
I hold her right
the one which still
responds to touch
so we may conduct
Maurizio Pollini, piano

Bar after bar
measure by measure
we lead the étude
her will to connect
never flagging
for three minutes
and forty seconds

But she is leaving
as music disappears
into memory

She is dying
slowly, but not too slowly

70

Breath

I.

Out of time, sad to say
Mother sank into
a Dog-Days' coma
at millennium's end
her murmuring heart
her labouring lungs
wound down, down, down
on August 4, 1999
her husband, Guy
her daughter, Kristen
in vigil waited
to bid her
Fare thee well, love
each breath less
than the breath before
     the breath before
         breath before
             before
the long, last *ex h a l e*

II.

In the hospital room
during the final days
Kristen had sought
her own meditation mat
her own meditation shawl
to rest on the floor
to accept the sorrow
of her mother's dying
of her partner Scott's
approaching death
by cancer
to focus on the breath
the holy incense of air

Prana   prana   prana

72

The Very Moment

While I waited outside
after library work-day
across the August campus
at clock-tower college
waited for my day-camp son
to logoff a computer
step over the threshold
and return with me home
one dark cloud floated above
westerly light warmed my face
bells chimed 4:45
and I was caught
joyously, damply
in sunfall rainshine
the very moment
my mother
died.

Dream-mother

Out of the spirit-west
beyond white cliffs
into impossible blue
above small Wiarton
dream-mother eagle arcs
through a silent circle
over shops and hotels
over wave-windy bay
over rock-cut road
she pauses to hover
marking the old Bluff
ancestral home once more
when her white feathers
at head and tail merge
lengthen and billow
she becomes holy chorist
soon   the soloist no more.

The Fee for Exaltation

a single chiming rise
sees a woman
her mouth
her sunlight
lingering
away
where traces
felled the soul
one gathered life
freely
morning
and light

points
right here
already consumed
offerings
in life
to laugh
surrounded
at zenith
a hazy memory
descent
past arms pointing
morning guides

upward
the sacred never ran
ever flew
even joyous
her spirit eyes
glass swirling
and crimson
die
like waves
and revels

with old rich links
in our own story
promised
committed
and scattered
by the weight
Mother crossed
books remain blue
and many texts
ghost
the loftiest streaks
the infinite past
souls imagine
how much
a strong and worthy
thousand words
to hold a holy

covenant
a deathbed dream
in deep
and darker
journey back
and again
remember
sacred water
spirit pilgrim
gave way to
sky delight
leaves distant earth
some of her
future

the voice
sometimes whispered
strength in her
behold your life
spilt easily
the same light
from birth
the will
never flagging
to rest
to accept
the dying
step over

and return
with one light
out beyond
impossible
small
arcs

Notes

"Rhymes with Orangeman" includes found elements from a 1915 revised version of the *Loyal Orange Association of British America: Rules of the Royal Scarlet Order, Constitution and Laws*, from Allan Bartley's 1987 book *Proud People: The Lindsay Township History Book*, and from *The Wiarton Echo*.

"Four Times Removed" mentions the nineteenth-century X Club, whose members (G. Busk, E. Frankland, T. A. Hirst, J. D. Hooker, T. H. Huxley, J. Lubbock, H. Spencer, W. Spottiswoode, and Tyndall) worked for the advancement of science. *Tyndall blue* refers to John Tyndall's scientific investigations into the diffraction of light in the sky (the *Tyndall effect*). William Tynedale, one of the first translators of *The Bible* into English, was burned at the stake for heresy in 1536.

"S(L)ight Plays upon Works by Cousin John, Scientist" is a wholly found poem with materials from Tyndall's *The Belfast Address* to The British Association for the Advancement of Science in 1874, *Hours of Exercise in the Alps* (one of his books on mountaineering), *On Sound* (one of his scientific experiments), and *Apology for the Belfast Address* (his response to criticism of his 1874 address).

"The Fee for Exaltation" is a wholly found poem with words from all the other poems in this collection, in order of their appearance.

I
Mother

II
Arid Zone A

III
Rhymes with Orangeman

IV
My Mummy's Dead

Notes

MEMBER OF SCABRINI GROUP

Québec, Canada
2007